RELIGIOUS LIVING

OF THE CLASSIC

K ON RELIGION

RELIGIOUS
LIVING

GEORGIA HARKNESS

Association Press · *New York*

201
H33

RELIGIOUS LIVING

Copyright ©️ 1957 by
National Board of Young Men's Christian As

Association Press, 291 Broadway, New York

All rights reserved, including the right of reproduc
tion in whole or in part in any form, under
International, Pan-American, and Universal Co
right Conventions.

3 8404
Oct. 1959

Fourth Printing, April 1959

Price, 50 cents

Library of Congress catalog card number: 57-5496

Printed in the United States of America

PREFACE

Our age is characterized by lack of a sense of direction. This manifests itself acutely in the uncertainty, frustration, and inner conflict that bring confusion into many lives and make this a day of nervous tension as well as of shifting morals. There are many causes of this situation, but none more influential than the secularization which has sapped the religious sense of life's meaning and drained off the resources for effective living which religion imparts. Many things need to be done for the reconstruction of contemporary life, but without a revitalizing of religion no widespread or lasting increase in personal stability can be expected.

This book is addressed to those persons who recognize—however dimly—that they ought not to be indifferent to religion but who do not know in what direction to move to lay hold upon it. It aims to suggest as simply as possible how to find religion and how to grow in religious power. No one realizes better than the author that this is a presumptuous undertaking. Religious living is never a merely human achievement and it is not to be reduced to rule. Yet some procedures are more likely than others to lead to a living experience of religion—and the need of a bewildered generation is urgent.

The foregoing paragraphs were written as the preface to the first edition of *Religious Living* when it appeared in the Hazen series. Given the opportunity twenty years later to write a new preface, I find that the same condition and the same need prevail, if anything in accented form. In spite of encouraging signs of a new religious interest, millions of persons still grope, and need more than anything else the stabilizing and sensitizing power of Christian faith.

Though I welcome the opportunity for revision afforded by republication among the Reflection Books, no very basic changes have been made. All biblical citations have been changed to the Revised Standard Version, and obviously dated references removed or brought up to date. The Bibliography has been considerably altered to include some excellent newer books. Here and there words and phrases have been changed in the text, and since the book was originally written mainly for college students the scope of its applicability has been broadened. Beyond these matters it stands much as it has been over the past two decades. The author's chief concern is that in some measure it may prove a guide to the discovery of that new life which God stands ever ready to impart to those who truly seek him.

GEORGIA HARKNESS

CONTENTS

RELIGIOUS LIVING

CHAPTER ONE

WHAT IS
RELIGIOUS LIVING?

"You cannot imagine how horribly I bore myself!" says Hedda Gabler in Ibsen's play. "O that I knew where I might find him!" cried Job. Religion is a response to the first of these exclamations in the mood of the second.

Religion is both a quest and an achievement. It is a movement of life which, by turning outward, enriches and deepens the inward areas of personality. But how is it to be recognized?

What Is Religious Personality?

Instead of giving a formal definition of religion I must ask you to think of the most genuinely religious person you know—preferably not some saint of history, but a living personality who seems to you unmistakably religious. Probably you do not know many such, but you can think of at least one. Unfortunately, I cannot hear you describe that person, but I think I know what you will say.

If your experience runs true to that of most people, you will select as a genuinely religious person one whose life is characterized by spiritual vitality and depth; one whose roots go deep with fruits in the whole of life; one who not only believes in God with his mind but commits his life to God's care and tries to do the will of God as he sees it. He is one who thinks of others before himself, interested in helping others to achieve their best, but with a tact which draws the line at meddlesomeness; one who accepts responsibility for work that is worth doing and carries it through in spite of difficulty; one who meets both the great crises and the petty annoyances of life with courage, calm, and a sense of direction. Such a person will not be bored with himself or with the world, for he will find too many interesting things waiting to be done. He will not lack friends, for his own friendliness will win them to him spontaneously. He may be and quite probably will be misunderstood, but misunderstanding will not quench his spirit. In a deep sense, he will be a happy person, though I doubt whether you thought about this when you chose him. In the truly great spirits there are other qualities so much more important that happiness is not what one thinks of first.

Such a person will not be perfect. If you know him well enough, you will be able to find flaws in him. But if he were selfish,

15

morose, arrogant, insincere, or easily upset by the disturbing things that occur in every person's life, I doubt whether you could think of him as the most religious person you know. By selecting him—or her—you have given evidence that you recognize religious living when you see it.

What Does Religion Do?

I must ask you another question. What do you want most? No two persons want exactly the same things, but unless you are a very exceptional person, there are certain things you are sure to want. Among them are health; money enough for reasonable comfort; a chance to marry the person you love; a good time; congenial friends; surroundings of beauty; knowledge; a chance to do the work that interests you most. Beneath and above these is something which everybody at least subconsciously wants, though he does not always know that he wants it. This is a sense of inner fulfillment.

If you have the last of these, the other eight values mentioned take on a very different color. You think then not so much of what you want as of what life wants of you, and in either their presence or their absence you are able to live happily and beautifully. It is the lack of this inner adequacy which is responsible for the disturbed state of mind of great numbers of persons.

No one needs to be told that these are troubled times. That there are many external sources of trouble is evident, but the fundamental cause is lack of inner moorings. The older foundations of personal stability have dissolved and we have not found new ones. There is no clearer evidence of this than the vogue of certain best sellers, the content of which can be reduced to the simple advice to get interested in somebody or something and stop being bored. The attempt to run away from oneself by alcohol and fast driving is a subconscious recognition that there is not much at the center of one's life to stay with.

Without religion, we are not likely to emerge from this confusion. Religious faith, paradoxically, does two things at once: it lifts one *out of* himself, and it reinforces one *in* himself. It directs attention toward God and toward other people and new centers of interest develop. Far from being the "escape from reality" some people call it, it normally heightens and intensifies one's power to grapple with reality. Art does this to some extent—so do human love and devotion to any cause which commands our loyalty. But nothing else does it so powerfully as religion, for nothing else has so high an object of devotion. Nothing else so well enables one "to see life steadily and see it whole," for no other interest is so inclusive.

To see more concretely what this means,

let us examine the difference religion makes in each of the things you want most. Religion relates to the whole of life, and therefore to all of them.

Work. To begin at the end of the list, we said that everybody wants a chance to do the work which interests him most. It would be folly to maintain that religion can guarantee it. It is a large part of the Christian enterprise so to remake society that everybody can have such work—but it will be a long time before this happens. In the meantime religion can help you to choose your vocation by a dependable purpose, and to find satisfaction in whatever vocation—or lack of it—you have to accept.

It is not everybody's duty to follow a vocation specifically labeled religious. Nothing much worse could be imagined than for every devout person, regardless of fitness, to decide to be a clergyman! There is perhaps as much need of Christians in politics as in pulpits. But every person ought to choose his vocation in the light of the most inclusive service he can give and in fidelity to his truest ideal of the way of God. Work thus chosen brings its own enrichment. Clement of Alexandria, in the second century, described with poetic insight the effect of religious vision upon the tasks of the common life:

Holding festival, then, in our whole life, persuaded that God is altogether on every side present, we cultivate our fields, praising; we sail the sea, hymning; in all the rest of our conversation we conduct ourselves according to rule.[1]

Still more is religion needed for steadiness of soul when you are forced either to be without work, or to work at something you greatly dislike. If you cannot get paid work to do, there is plenty of useful volunteer service which needs to be done in every com-

[1] *Stromata*, VII, 7 in *Ante-Nicene Fathers*, Vol. II, p. 533.

munity, and a religious incentive will help you to find it. And no work which you must do is drudgery if you have vision enough to see in it a God-given duty, or a contribution to the happiness and welfare of other persons. It is sentimentality to claim that this is easy when the persons are distant and unknown; it is blasphemy to make this an excuse for complacency about the toil of underprivileged workers. But the thought is invigorating when applied to one's own work. There is no occupation, however interesting, that does not require certain monotonous, humdrum chores to be done; and possibly it is in these, more than anywhere else, that one needs the religious sense of a larger meaning. Martin Luther suggested that the maid who sweeps a room or the man who milks the cows might do so to the glory of God—and the same principle holds of pounding the typewriter and answering the telephone.

Knowledge. Among everybody's "wants"

we listed knowledge. This means that everybody wants to know at least enough to "get along in the world." It certainly does not mean that everybody is avid for an education! The schools and colleges are full of people who are not. One reason for this is a decline in the seriousness of intellectual purpose which the Christian religion in earlier days imparted.

When one begins to condemn religion for being obscurantist and reactionary, one needs to remember that it was religion which kept intellectual culture alive in the Middle Ages, religion which led to the founding of the greater number of colleges in this country, and religion through the missionary enterprise which has been the chief educational agency in large sections of the world. Religion does not directly impart knowledge any more than it guarantees employment. But in somewhat parallel fashion, wholesome religion makes the spread of education a social duty, and it gives to individuals who take it seriously enough an incentive to pursue learning with zest and direction. If you are in school and can see no reason for being there, perhaps this means that your religion is weak, though other things also may be the matter. For some persons whom I know who could not go to college, religion has transformed plain, rebellious discontent into a "divine discontent" driving them to self-education and the enrichment of life.

Beauty. Religion and beauty are very closely allied. Some who think they have never had a religious experience have really had one through beauty without knowing it. If you have ever felt your spirit lifted and enlarged in the presence of a great canyon or waterfall, or a majestic storm, or a flaming sunset, or the soft hush of summer twilight, or the play of northern lights, or the flashing of stars in illimitable distances—then you ought not to say carelessly that you have never had a religious experience. If you have ever sensed something holy in a baby's smile or an old man's face, in an early morning bird song or a great oratorio, in Beethoven's Hymn to Joy or in a forest of great pines whose music lets one understand the legend of the Aeolian harp, then the presumption is strong that you have grasped something of the meaning of worship.

But it is by no means certain that you have. An aesthetic experience, even though it moves you deeply, is not necessarily worship. Worship occurs when you feel yourself in the presence of that Power upon which you and the universe depend. When you perceive, however dimly, that you and this Power are *together* and you feel yourself both small and great before this presence, then you are worshiping. You become aware of its "worth-ship." Wordsworth could describe this experience better than most of us, and he said:

> I have felt
> A presence that disturbs me with the joy
> Of elevated thoughts: a sense sublime
> Of something far more deeply interfused,
> Whose dwelling is the light of setting suns,
> And the round ocean and the living air,
> And the blue sky, and in the mind of man.

This is one of life's greatest experiences, and anyone who has not felt it has less than a fully rounded personality.

Friendship. It is possible to have about friendship the same sort of high illumination. It is desirable that we should, and something is wrong if we do not, at least occasionally, sense the holiness of human affections. To use other persons simply as means to achieving our ends, as we have a right to do with *things,* is to treat persons as things. This is the surest way to sever a friendship, not simply because the other person resents it, but for the deeper reason that it assaults the sacredness of human relations. Jesus perceived with greater insight than anyone else who ever lived the religious nature of human fellowship. He treated everybody as a friend, and laid upon his disciples the obligation to do likewise. The highest tribute recorded as spoken by him was, "You are my friends."[2]

If friendship is a holy relation, it follows naturally that the religious person is better able than another to experience deep and lasting friendship. Even Aristotle, who lacked Jesus' religious insight, repudiated as merely secondary and impermanent the friendships based on utility and pleasure, and said that perfect friendships could exist only between good men who in their virtues had something to share.[3]

It is clear that friendship is one of the most important expressions of religion, and religion one of the most important foundations of friendship. But I do not believe, as some do, that they can be identified. Religion is more

[2] John 15: 14.
[3] *Nichomachean Ethics*, VIII, iii.

than human fellowship. As with beauty, there is a close and sometimes inseparable connection; yet an experience is *religious* only when it takes in the larger Reality that makes possible all friendship and all living.

Play. One of our most natural desires is for a good time. Everybody has to play in some way for his mental health, though one person's manner of play might be torture to another. It is unfortunate that churches ever placed a ban on wholesome recreations, for without some interest pursued for sheer enjoyment, one's personality turns inward to become distorted and morose.

But not all recreations are wholesome. How can we tell the difference? There are three simple rules by which to know, though the application is not always simple. Ask yourself these questions about any form of play. Will it do you harm, now or in the future, overtly or subtly? Will it harm anyone else, either directly or by your example? Will it,

27

by claiming time or energy that ought to go elsewhere, cut you off from some greater good? If you can answer "no" without deluding yourself, go ahead.

Yet recreation is not enough to make people happy. There is plenty of recreation available—chances to dance, to dine, to play cards, to go to the movies, to watch the television—and yet people in general are not enjoying themselves. The richness of life essential to inner peace comes only from an "integrated personality." Life's greatest integrating force is Christian faith. The most religious persons I know are also the happiest persons, for they have the outward satisfactions of others without the inward dissatisfactions of worry, discontent, or "the blues."

Home. You want to have a home. Every young person desires to marry, unless his personality is warped or he has strong interests which cannot be pursued in conjunction with marriage. It is well that people now admit this frankly instead of, as in the past, acting as if there were something immodest about it.

Do you expect to be married by a minister? The chances are that you do. Do you expect to attend church afterward? Of that I am not so sure, although it is encouraging that more young couples attend church now than formerly. Do you expect to have your baby baptized? Do you expect to send your children to Sunday School? I am not confident that you do, but I think perhaps this is more likely than that you will go regularly yourself. If death enters your home, you will ask the help of a minister.

The point of these questions is that, however much you may turn your back on the church, you will call upon it in those aspects of your life most vital to you. The late Dean Sperry wrote graphically, "In obedience to

29

some deep unreasoned prompting, men seek churches when life is most real."[4]

There is a difference—and a very large difference—between turning to the institutions of religion in a crucial event, and making religion the constant undergirding of your family life. Without the second, the first degenerates often into barren ceremony; with it, marriage is set far ahead in its prospects of happy fruition. This is why it is so important to choose as one's mate a person of kindred religious interests. There is no place where the tensions and strains of living are harder than in the intimate relations of a home, and no sphere which has greater need of deep-rooted religious fellowship. With more religion there would be fewer ill-considered marriages and fewer broken homes.

But before you can marry you have to see something in sight to live on. People some-

[4] *Reality in Worship* (New York: Macmillan, 1925), p. 30.

times forget that love will not pay the grocer
—but with tragic consequences. What has religion to do with money?

Money. An old Hebraic idea, in which unfortunately many people still believe, is that
prosperity is a mark of divine favor, bestowed
upon "the better element" because of superior
ability or virtue. Under cover of it, all manner of exploitation has been justified. An
equally false, though perhaps less pernicious,
error is the notion that wealth is inherently
evil. What Jesus taught is that "the cares of
the world and the delight in riches" corrupt
the soul. This is because obsession with things
ruins one's scale of values and puts profits and
possessions above reverence for personality.

What the Christian religion does about
money is twofold. First, if your religion is
real, it will affect your money getting, money
spending, money giving. The biblical parable
of the talents[5] suggests aptly, by a word which

[5] Matthew 25: 14-30.

31

to us has a double meaning, the importance of viewing both our money and our ability as something entrusted to us by God. And second, unless you greatly lack vision, your religion will make you feel the urgent necessity of changing a world situation which denies to many millions of hungry people the basic material foundations of life. If your religion does not have both these effects, there is something wrong with it.

Health. We have been moving backward through the list of things which everybody wants. And the first of these was health. Religion is very intimately related to health—first to mental health, and then through mental to physical well-being. The author of one of the Hebrew proverbs knew centuries ago what psychologists have recently been affirming: "A cheerful heart is a good medicine, but a downcast spirit dries up the bones."[6] Religion is the chief begetter of cheerful

[6] Proverbs 17: 22.

hearts and the chief lifter of downcast spirits. There is no getting around such testimony as that of a great psychologist, Dr. Carl Jung, who writes,

Among all my patients in the second half of life—that is to say, over thirty-five—there has not been one whose problem in the last resort was not that of finding a religious outlook on life. It is safe to say that every one of them fell ill because he had lost that which the living religions of every age have given to their followers, and none of them has been really healed who did not regain his religious outlook.[7]

But more important than what religion does in restoring health is the power it imparts to live courageously in the absence of it. Without a religious faith, there is sheer unmitigated evil in the writhing and torment to be discerned in any hospital. With it, anything can be endured and transcended. When it enables a young man losing his arm through

[7] *Modern Man in Search of a Soul* (New York: Harcourt, Brace and Company, 1933), p. 264.

another's carelessness to sing about the goodness of life and of people, a girl facing incurable blindness to readjust her life without bitterness, a woman confronting sure death from cancer to live usefully in the present and view the future without flinching, then religion gives power.

Religion ought never to be used merely as a tool to the acquisition of health, or wealth, or any other value. This is not why it exists. But if God and other persons are put at the center of one's life, one's own personality becomes thereby enriched and healed. This is part of the meaning of the great paradox in the words of Jesus, "For whoever would save his life will lose it, and whoever loses his life for my sake will find it."[8] In a tense and restless quest of panaceas for happiness, hosts of people are now seeking to save their lives— and are losing them in sordidness and discontent. In worthful self-giving and steady

[8] Matthew 16: 25; Mark 8: 35; Luke 9: 24.

reliance upon God, others are finding sources of power for the sudden crises and steady tensions of life, and are proving in their experience the truth of the word of the prophet, "In returning and rest you shall be saved; in quietness and in trust shall be your strength."[9]

These are some of the differences religion makes in life. Because it makes them, it is the major need of this day, as it has been of every day. But its gifts are not to be purchased by wishful thinking. They are to be won by the surrender of all that one has.

Religious living requires a firsthand discovery of God. This means much more than finding arguments by which to prove that God exists. It means worshiping God in humility of spirit and submitting—for a lifetime —in moral obedience to his demands. If you are not willing that this cost you something, you should read no further.

[9] Isaiah 30: 15.

CHAPTER TWO

OBSTACLES TO
RELIGIOUS LIVING

The kind of religious living described in the preceding chapter is not reserved for great saints, past or present, or for the cloister. Under its attractive power I have seen a person censorious and unpopular because of a lashing tongue become considerate, co-operative, and spontaneously beloved; one drifting without personal or vocational objective get a purpose which transformed scattered energy into concentrated power; one unhappy and morose almost to the point of suicide become triumphant; one immature and childish become full-grown. I have seen a girl with infantile paralysis able through Christian faith to face the prospect of being a cripple all her days; one whose life was shattered to its depths by a broken engagement pull together the pieces to go on with serenity; one who had crushing family burdens bear them without being overwhelmed. Religion makes selfish people unselfish, disorganized people integrated, fearful people brave, weak people strong.

If it does these things, why does not everybody appropriate its gifts? The answer lies partly in certain obstacles. Let us examine these to see how they thwart religious living.

The Secular Environment

It is an unwarranted escape from reality to suppose that our environment makes it impossible to lay hold upon the power of God for religious living. Yet it is required both by wisdom in viewing ourselves and by tolerance in viewing others that we should realize the difficulties presented by the environment.

Religion has hard sledding in the modern world because we live in a *thing-centered civilization.* Jesus made God and human personality the supreme objects of devotion; our society does not. His interests were primarily in *worth,* not in *use,* and as a consequence he was appreciative of persons while we are possessive of things. Religion affects but is also affected by moral attitudes, and a depersonalized society is bound to be an ethically insensitive and an irreligious society. Our economic system, centered in the amassing of profits for private gain, too often thwarts spiritual values by producing exploitation and arrogance on one side of the chasm, bitterness and dull misery on the other.

The thing-centered nature of our environment crops out everywhere in the tendency

to judge the desirability of a vocation or position by probable income, to judge successful
living by the acquisition of material comforts,
to judge the attractiveness of recreation or
possessions by the things advertised on every
billboard or radio or television program. It is
neither possible nor desirable to return to the
pre-industrial simplicity of the peasant society
in which Jesus lived. But the standards of
value which he there enumerated and lived
by—the holiness of God; the equality of all
men before God; the duty to treat all men as
neighbors and brothers; the blessedness of
living in simplicity, sympathy, humility, aspiration, mercy, purity, peace, and steadfast
devotion to high convictions[1]—these are as
important today as ever. They are very difficult to maintain in a secular civilization
which, in obsession with things, presses upon
us from every side to jostle them out of con-
sciousness.

[1] Matthew 5: 3-10.

A second obstacle to religious living in our secular environment is *nationalism in conjunction with militarism*. In general terms, one may admit readily enough that God is to be worshiped before the state. But in a concrete situation has one the courage, if his convictions lead him to think compulsory military training wrong, to refuse to participate in it? to say what one believes about military force at the risk of offending influential people? I do not say that absolute pacifism is the only Christian attitude to take toward war, or that one's conscience will necessarily lead one in this direction. But it is always required of a Christian that he put his conscience above an edict of the state which he judges to be un-Christian, and this is not easy to do. God calls us to be loyal citizens of our own country, but also to love and to serve all men, viewing all as our brothers because we are all sons of the one Father. To put the state above our religious loyalties means that we are not obeying the first commandment, "You shall have no other gods before me."

The state is not the only group which demands primacy of loyalty and sets up strange gods. One's fraternity or club or a particular group of friends may do exactly the same, and do it with an immediacy that makes its effects the more devastating. Campus or community politics may have in them all the self-seeking, petty arrogance, and propulsion toward petty loyalties which one finds in the politics of a state—and religious organizations are not devoid of this tendency. Until one faces these unpleasant facts and sets his will toward living by his convictions instead of being a puppet of his group, he will not be ready to achieve religious living.

A third foe of religion in our present environment is *dissipation of energies through pressure of time*. We live at high speed, partly because we have to and partly because we

like it. To spend much time in spiritual medi-
tation seems almost impossible when one
must race from the time the alarm clock rings
to get into one's clothes, snatch a bit of break-
fast, catch a bus, rush around all day about
one's work or other engagements, and in general keep going from morning till too late at
night to get enough sleep. In this tempo the
"morning watch" of earlier days has gone the
way of the family altar. But that some time
be taken for relaxation of spirit is indispensable to religious living.

As time presses upon us, so does *space*.
"Religion is what the individual does with
his own solitariness."[2] By this, Alfred North
Whitehead meant much more than physical
solitariness, but to have some of the latter is
essential. And we do not have much of it. If
you live with other people, it is not always
easy to "go into your room and shut the door

2 *Religion in the Making* (New York: Cambridge University Press, 1936), p. 16.

and pray to your Father,"[3] and in most dormitories to room alone is no guarantee of privacy. Walter Rauschenbusch wrote simply and devoutly,

> In the castle of my soul
> Is a little postern gate,
> Whereat, when I enter,
> I am in the presence of God.

But for many people today there is no castle of the soul—only an open highway along which whiz all sorts of fast-moving vehicles.

These barriers to religious living—economic, political, temporal, and spatial—are real difficulties. It is easy to say, "What can you do about them?" and assume that you can do nothing.

As aspects of the total system of things in which we live, no single individual can do much about them. One must keep working to change bad external situations, knowing that

[3] Matthew 6: 6.

the change will come slowly if at all. But in regard to personal religious living, there the situation is different. It is possible, not to live perfectly, but to live without letting possessions or group loyalties become one's God, without letting either the rush or the community of life push out the worship of God. Some people do, and they demonstrate the possibility. But it is no easy achievement, and one must believe very much that it is worth while before he will make the effort.

Disintegration of Belief

Thus far I have not said much about intellectual belief. But this is not because belief is unimportant. It is a superficial judgment to say, "It does not matter what you believe as long as you live right." It matters immensely, both to one's thinking and to one's living. Our morals come to us largely through social conditioning, and we acquire habits unreflectively; but we change them when we believe the old ones to be wrong or foolish. A course in philosophy will not make a person religious, but a wrong philosophy may undermine one's religion and one's life by shattering the foundations of belief on which religion rests.

There is no single closed system of beliefs that a religious person must accept. As there is a diversity of gifts among Christians,[4] so is there room for diversity of opinion on many matters. Religious people have not always been tolerant, for they have had convictions —and one of the hardest things in the world is to combine tolerance with conviction. But it is also one of the most necessary. A primary foe of religion is spiritual arrogance, and arrogance roots in the belief that one's own way is the right way and the other person's wrong. To believe that one is right as far as one can see without condemning another for differing—this is an intellectual and personal

[4] Ephesians 4: 11-16.

attitude of very great importance to religious living.

Wide as is the range of possible diversity, there are four beliefs which seem to me to constitute a religious minimum. Without these, religion cannot stand—not because of any creedal necessity, but because of the nature of religion itself. In their absence, something goes out which is essential to its life. One may cut off a finger, a hand, or an arm and still live—but one cannot lose a brain or a heart and survive. These four beliefs are religion's vital organs.

The basic religious minimum is *belief in a God who elicits devotion and obedience*. The need of a sustaining Power to rely upon in human weakness has been mentioned. But, important though this is, it is not the main reason that religion requires God. Religion causes useful things to happen in a person's life and in society. But religion is not primarily an instrument; it is an attitude of appreciation. As true friendship does not come from using another person, but from loving him and feeling his worth, so true religion does not arise from using God but from realizing God's worth.[5] The psalm[6] which begins

> God is our refuge and strength,
>   a very present help in trouble,

rises to a climax in

> "Be still, and know that I am God:
>   I am exalted among the nations,
>   I am exalted in the earth!"

This is not the place to survey all the reasons for believing in God. For some persons, the fact that God is the central certainty of our Hebrew-Christian heritage, revealed supremely in the life of Jesus, is enough. Others feel the need of further philosophical inquiry, and for these there are books available to

[5] The derivation of the word worship is the Anglo-Saxon *weorthscipe*, which means worth-ship.

[6] Psalm 46.

guide their thinking.[7] Among the facts which point to God's existence are the marvelous orderliness of physical nature and the creative evolutionary advance of which science gives increasing evidence; the nature of human personality—inexplicable unless a higher personality is its source; the pervasive power of religious experience in all ages, which in spite of some hideous aberrations has nevertheless been dominantly on the side of goodness, beauty, and truth. Perhaps the triumphant living of great personalities who have staked their lives on God's existence and the acceptance of his moral demands gives clearest evidence, for here belief and living meet. However such belief is arrived at, it is important to have it—and equally important to have it without dogmatism and without indifference to its implications.

The second requirement is *belief in spiritual personality*. This does not mean that one

[7] See list, page 121.

has to believe in a soul separable from a body. But unless one believes that he is something more than a piece of physical matter operating mechanically and driven by blind forces, he will not think it worth while to try to worship or to guide his destiny by ideals.

In a famous and beautifully written essay, *A Free Man's Worship*, Bertrand Russell called upon us to realize that man is simply "the outcome of accidental collocations of atoms."[8] He observes:

> To take into the inmost shrine of the soul the irresistible forces whose puppets we seem to be—death and change, the irrevocableness of the past, and the powerlessness of man before the blind hurry of the universe from vanity to vanity —to feel these things and know them is to conquer them.[9]

This is an heroic statement of a materialistic philosophy. But examine its consistency. If man were simply the powerless puppet of

8 (Golden Book, 1934, Reprint).
9 *Ibid.*, p. 23.

ought. Man is more than nature; he is less than God.

As religion asserts man's power as a spiritual being to choose his destiny, so it asserts man's need of superhuman resources to achieve his destiny. Only as man sees his sin and weakness and turns in humility to a higher power can he really be great. Only as he casts out all lesser gods to exalt in his life the God of love does he find himself adequate to living in a world of moral conflict.

In *Thus Spake Zarathustra,* Nietzsche represents Zarathustra as talking to an old saint of the forest who had not yet heard that the gods were dead. They had laughed themselves to death over the idea of there being only one God![11]

"Dead are all the Gods: now do we desire the Superman to live,"[12] he makes his hero

[11] *Op. cit.,* Discourse LII. *Works,* ed., Levy, 1909, Vol. XI, p. 222.
[12] *Ibid.,* p. 91. Discourse XXII.

say. Through Nietzsche's own influence and that of many others, this has come near to happening in the thought of modern times. Whenever men are exalted to a position of supremacy and many gods possess men's lives, human self-sufficiency causes the sense of God's reality to fade. The evolutionary optimism of the nineteenth century and the humanism of the twentieth not only placed too high an estimate on man's powers, but they gave support to those who called God an amusing relic of a superstitious age. Partly through the tragic events that have shattered such self-confidence, partly through more constructive movements in religious thought, this mood is now less prevalent than formerly.

The fourth essential is both a belief and an attitude. It is *the conviction that personal religion is both possible and desirable.* This point need not be dwelt upon, for it is implied in everything said thus far. However well thought out one's system of beliefs may be, despair or indifference regarding the possibility of religion will cause religious experience to die at the roots before it starts to grow.

In stating such a minimum of religious belief, I have not intended to suggest that no other beliefs are important. There is no maximum, for both in living and in thinking the possibilities are inexhaustible. There are other concepts about which one needs to think, including some matters that are very vital to Christian faith. Among these are the Bible and its interpretation, the relations of religion to science, the divinity of Jesus and what there is about him that makes him our moral leader and saviour, the meaning of the cross, the Christian hope of immortality.[13] One needs to consider not only whether God ex-

[13] The reader will find further discussion of these aspects of Christian belief in my book of theology for laymen, *Understanding the Christian Faith*.

ists, but what sort of God Jesus reveals and calls us to worship and serve. One needs to ask what is a religious person's social obligation in a world full of evil. All these and more one needs to think about, and I shall later discuss some of these matters. But in all these, there is room for disagreement among persons sincerely Christian. The four beliefs mentioned in this section—a God to worship and rely upon, spiritual personality, human inadequacy, and confidence that religion is possible and worth while—these are the indispensable foundations of religious experience, whether Christian, Jewish, or any other kind. In their absence, religion disappears to pass over into a type of social adjustment or altruistic ethics which may be very good but is not *religion*.

These concepts ought not to be believed in simply as instruments to religious experience. Truth, like religion, can stand on its own feet—and there is no chasm between them. ". . . you will know the truth, and the truth will make you free"[14]—free from intolerance and flippancy, free from haunting fears that you are deceiving yourself for the sake of an emotional glow. No one need ever be afraid to walk up to religious truth and look it in the face, for it will not quail and slink away before honest scrutiny.

Personal Attitudes

The effect of religious faith and devotion is to give one the kind of personal attitudes described in the first chapter. Is it necessary, then, to presuppose that one have these attitudes in order to find religion?

Certainly not all of them. It would be reasoning in a circle to say that one must first be unselfish, integrated, courageous, and self-controlled before he can appropriate the power to live in this way. Yet, unless our wills are set in the right direction, we are power-

[14] John 8: 32.

less to move in that direction. God does not thrust his gifts on anybody.

The quest for God is compatible with much sin and weakness—else none could enter upon it. Yet some attitudes by their nature shut off the quest.

The first of these is *indifference.* If you do not care whether or not you live religiously, you certainly will not so live. You will make no effort to overcome obstacles set by the environment or to acquire a dependable set of beliefs. You will simply go on drifting. If people were as fainthearted about their athletics and their courtships as they often are about their religion, there would not be many high scores made or fair ladies won!

The second is *arrogance.* If you think that you are good enough as you are, you will make no effort to be better. If you think you are as good as other people around you, setting up some ordinary human standard as a criterion, you will feel no impulse to grow

57

"to mature manhood, to the measure of the stature of the fullness of Christ."[15]

A third is *insincerity*. If you think you can put religion on and off like your clothes, dressing up for special occasions, you will not be able to find it when you want it. Religion is not this kind of outer wrapping. It is something that grows from the inside outward, never something "put on."

What this means is simple to state, not simple to execute. Before you can lay hold upon divine resources for triumphant living, you must be in earnest about needing them, humble in your receptivity, sincere in your quest. You must be willing to submit to self-discipline, claiming no alibis and shunning no demand which your best insights set before you. Finding a religion to live by is no easy matter. The Christian religion is the hardest of all, for it has a cross at its center. But if you make the quest earnestly, and with hu-

[15] Ephesians 4: 13.

mility and sincerity measure up to the conditions, achievement is certain; for God is dependable. If not, like the rich young ruler in the Bible,[16] you may go away sorrowful, having great possessions of self-interest but unwilling to pay the price.

[16] Matthew 19: 16-22.

CHAPTER THREE

BEGINNINGS IN RELIGIOUS LIVING

It is a deep and abiding insight of the Christian faith that all discovery of God comes to us as a divine gift. Yet it is a gift which we cannot receive unless we lay hold upon it, meeting the conditions God imposes. In this chapter we shall inquire further what these conditions are and how best to meet them.

Meeting the Conditions

The factors already stated as obstacles to religious living could be turned around and stated as requirements. We are kept from religious living by the pressure of economic interests, rival loyalties, too little time, and not enough privacy: religious living requires an earnest attempt to live without letting things or people press too much upon us. Our religion is shaken at its foundations by too little or too much confidence in man, by disintegration of faith in God's existence or in the possibility of finding him: we move toward a constructive religious experience when we can accept at least these beliefs—and presumably more—with intellectual sincerity. We are shut out from the quest before we start if we are indifferent, arrogant, or insincere: in the spirit of earnest, humble search, God already begins to reveal himself to us. There is great truth in the words which Pascal represents God as saying, "Thou wouldst not have sought me hadst thou not already found me."

These things we need to do; these attitudes

we need to have. But this is not all. We live in a dependable universe. If this were not so, you could not put one foot ahead of the other to walk across a room. Suppose the muscular and neural co-ordinations on which you have depended since you were about a year old should suddenly fail you, and when you thought you were going to walk forward you began to go backward, or sprawl sidewise, or hit the ceiling! You do not expect this to happen, for you know that the laws of gravitation, friction, and tension by which walking takes place remain constant. Quite conceivably you may fall when you expect to walk—most people do at one time or another. But if you do, it will not be because anything gets out of gear in the universe. It will be either because something goes wrong in you, or because a slippery pavement or something to trip over suddenly presents a set of circumstances with which you are not co-ordinated.

There is a parable of religious living here.

God's spiritual forces, like his laws in nature, are dependable, though in a more subtle and personal sense which makes it impossible to state them in mathematical formulae. When you do what God wills, he is ready to help you to go forward. He wills that you learn to "stand on your own feet" and go ahead in reliance upon his inexhaustible resources— never in overweening self-confidence.

This is a very old analogy, for one of the most beautiful pieces of imagery in the writings of the prophets is that in which Hosea represents God as saying to the people of Israel:

> When Israel was a child, I loved him,
>   and out of Egypt I called my son. . . .
>
> It was I who taught Ephraim to walk,
>   I took them up in my arms;
>   but they did not know that I healed them.
> I led them with cords of compassion,
>   with the bands of love. . . .[1]

[1] Hosea 11: 1-4.

This metaphor of the spiritual life bursts through the limits of so slow and earthly a process as walking and rises on great wings in the words of Isaiah:

They who wait for the Lord shall renew their
    strength,
  they shall mount up with wings like eagles,
they shall run and not be weary,
they shall walk and not faint.[2]

Since this is just what the great religious spirits described in the first chapter do, there must be a way. What are the conditions which must be met before one can walk, or run, or "mount up" in a spiritual sense? The analogy can be carried further.

First, *before you walk at all you must have a stimulus.* This need not be from without, though it usually is. It may be the idea that you need exercise, or simply the feeling in you that you want to move. But more often, something outside attracts you. You go to

[2] Isaiah 40: 31.

your meals, or go to a store, or go after the ball in a game because you want to get something. Sometimes the stimulus makes you want to avoid something—you run because you are afraid, or you dislike being alone and you seek companionship. Some stimuli are more potent than others, some more laudable than others—but there is always a stimulus of some kind present wherever there is activity.

In the religious life also, you take steps toward the discovery of God only through a stimulus. You may do so from a conscious sense of need or from some deep inner impulse which you cannot clearly define. Usually, however, it happens when something of great worth attracts you or when the fear or loneliness of life overwhelms you. But, however it comes, *without a stimulus there is no response*.

A second condition to be met if one would walk is to *do something about the things that*

65

are in the way. When you are moving to a new place, whether at school or camp or into a new home, your possessions get into what Shakespeare called a "most admired disorder." Your things are in a mess, and you wonder what you are ever going to do with them all! Meanwhile you have to keep living —and that means you have to walk around them, climb over them, or put them away. To walk around them is only a temporary expedient that settles nothing, and to keep doing so long is nerve-racking. To climb over them may sometimes be necessary, but it impedes progress and consumes energy. The only sensible thing for you to do is to get your things into livable order, throwing away what is useless, keeping what you need, possibly putting some in storage.

The application to religious living is simple. Everybody has about him many things that clutter up his life—impulses to selfishness, to acquisitiveness, to the love of power and prestige, to the misuse of sex, to irritability, faultfinding, jealousy, laziness, carelessness, irresponsibility. These sins are mixed chaotically with other things we should not want to dispense with, and they cause an unlovely and uncomfortable disorder. To stumble over them is painful and to walk around them futile—the only sensible thing is to clear them out to make a place for what is worth keeping. Only so can we have the beauty of ordered living. The Bible says something about housecleaning, as about most things. It tells of a man who cleaned house so indiscriminately, sweeping out the good with the evil, that the evil spirit that went out returned with seven others.[3] This is not the way to get order and progress. *Without a clearing away of evil there is no orderly goodness.*

A third condition to be met in order to walk is to *keep one foot on the ground and the other off.* If you keep both feet down, you

[3] Luke 11: 24-26.

cannot move unless you are dragged. If you try to keep both off, you can stay up a few seconds by a jump or a hop, but the pull of the earth will inevitably bring you down. Most of us walk a good many miles during our lives without thinking of this, but no baby could ever learn to walk who did not discover it by experience.

This simple fact, transferred to the religious sphere, has very great significance. It symbolizes the need of uniting realism with idealism, nature with supernature, immanence with transcendence, time with eternity. Any theology which emphasizes one of these terms to the exclusion of the other either becomes "of the earth, earthy" or moves in the clouds. The Christian religion, more than any other approach to life, makes it possible to synthesize these otherwise contrary concepts. It keeps close to human living and human needs, but it does so through an incentive and source of power which are more than human. *Without divine power there is no human achievement.*

A fourth condition is *the need of regular exercise for efficiency and growth.* It is one of the simplest of physiological facts that un-used muscles tend to atrophy. The reason our walking muscles do not usually fail us, even after long illness, is that we use them so much in health. To have them not merely function but function well and grow in power, they must be used. An old story is told of a man who paid good money to learn to swim by correspondence but who drowned the first time he went in the water.

This need of action for health and growth has its religious meaning. Reading this book will not make anyone religious. Nor will read-ing any other book, even as great a book as the Bible. Nor will listening to a sermon. Nor will any kind of theoretical education or evan-gelistic technique. These agencies are not use-less and may be very valuable guides to religious living. But as substitutes for meeting the basic condition they are futile. The only thing that can lead to religious living is to submit one's will to God and then act according to the best light one can get. *Without action there is no growth.*

Steps in Religious Awakening

The historic term for the appropriation of religion is conversion. It is a good term, for it means in its derivation a "turning about"— from a self-centered to a God-centered life. That is just what happens in genuine religion. But the word has been spoiled for many people by the idea that a person gets converted only through some kind of hysterical revivalism, or that a person must suddenly change from a great sinner to something very different. Both are false, but since they linger still, we shall speak of "religious awakening" instead of "conversion." This means much the same but suggests also that without religion one is still asleep to the beauty and power of living.

Does everybody need a religious awakening? Do not people reared in an atmosphere of religion and culture live well enough without it? The answer is that everybody does need to wake up and live with new commitment to the way of God. This need not be a chaotic, soul-splitting experience, though it may be. It must be a soul-uniting, soul-deepening experience. It may be a sudden and dramatic or a gradual process, but it must be a decisive one. To some people new light comes, as to Paul on the Damascus road,[4] with blinding power. To others, in the daily tasks of life there comes a new sense of the sacredness of life and the dignity of God-given duty which makes one feel, "The place on which you are standing is holy ground,"[5] and afterward everything—nature, people,

4 Acts 22: 6-21.
5 Exodus 3: 1-12.

work—looks different. There are many "varieties of religious experience,"[6] and it is dogmatic to claim that one's own way is the only way—but they all have common elements.

To find one's way into living religion is the most important thing any person can do. There are four essential steps, corresponding to the four conditions just outlined. The first three have to do with beginnings; the fourth repeats these—for living religiously is a lifetime task—and adds much more. The steps are *awareness of need, repentance, surrender, growth.*

Awareness of Need. It was stated in surveying the conditions that *without a stimulus there is no response.* What the stimulus does in the appropriation of religion is to give us the awareness that we need it.

Occasionally, though not very often, this stimulus comes in the form of intellectual

---

[6] William James's great book by this title remains the classic description of types.

reflection upon life and its meaning. Professor Hoxie N. Fairchild relates in his book, *Toward Belief*, how his revival of interest in religion came about through attempting to set down in some philosophical dialogues his basic attitudes toward life—an attempt which led to the discovery that he "could not philosophize at all except from premises which were essentially religious."[7] But it comes in this way to few, and though religion may have an intellectual stimulus it is never wholly an intellectual matter.

At the opposite extreme, perhaps, lies the experience of the person whose awareness of need comes as a result of inner impulses. Reason or an external stimulus may be involved, but he is not conscious of this. He feels as if he were being pursued by some power not himself, yet in himself, which he cannot evade or forget. The psalmist had this feeling when he cried out:

[7] (New York: Macmillan Company, 1935), viii.

Whither shall I go from thy Spirit?
Or whither shall I flee from thy presence?[8]

A classic statement of this experience is in
Francis Thompson's *The Hound of Heaven*:[9]

I fled Him, down the nights and down the days;
I fled Him, down the arches of the years;
I fled Him, down the labyrinthine ways
Of my own mind; and in the midst of tears
I hid from Him, and under running laughter.
Up vistaed hopes I sped;
And shot, precipitated,
Adown Titanic glooms of chasmèd fears,
From those strong Feet that followed, followed
after
But with unhurrying chase,
And unperturbèd pace,
Deliberate speed, majestic instancy,
They beat—and a Voice beat
More instant than the Feet—
"All things betray thee, who betrayest Me."

To most people the awareness of need
comes in neither so reasoned nor so impulsive

[8] Psalm 139: 7.
[9] Dodd, Mead & Company, New York. Quoted by
permission.

a way, but through some outside human
agency. This does not mean that God is not
present, for God works in us through persons,
things, and events. The stimulus may be an
address, a sermon, a service of worship, a
conversation or discussion, a conference, a
course, a book, a poem, a contact with some
strong religious personality, an enlarging
friendship, great religious music, an unusual
scene in nature or art, the presence of human
need, a new responsibility such as marriage
or parenthood, a transition to a new vocation
or to new surroundings, an important decision
to make, illness, danger, the death of someone loved—in fact, almost anything which
stirs us out of our complacency to make us
think more seriously about life. The stimulus
may be something happening once; it may
be a growing influence; it may be a combina-
tion of several factors, either all at once or
over a long period. But however it happens,

75

something must "stab our spirits broad awake."

What this means is that if you have already begun to have intimations that religion asks and offers something, you should deliberately expose yourself to the influences best suited to deepen this impression. There is no uniform rule as to which of these is best for you. You will have to discover experimentally, or let some wise counselor guide you. Those in the earlier part of the foregoing list are for everybody; others, such as illness and death, are not to be courted, but accepted with deepened insight when they come. The important thing is that you must staunchly refuse to let your inner self be drugged into lethargy and coma.

We have been speaking of the human agencies that stir in us a sense of need for religious faith. But these should in no sense be taken as a substitute for God's supreme gift—the revelation of himself in Jesus Christ for our light and our salvation. It is He who has led the way and who gives us power to respond to the love of God. All these other channels are but ways by which our lives are opened to him.

The primary agencies by which we are made aware of our need of Christ are the Church, the Bible, prayer, the living influence of other Christians, service to human need in response to the call of God. Since these are avenues to *growth* as well as *discovery*, we shall say more about them in the next chapter. But it must be said here that although one may turn his back on any of these, it is a sign of his own ethical and spiritual dullness if he does. There is rarely a church service, however poorly conducted, from which one cannot get some religious value if he will take to it a seeking and not a critical spirit. The Bible is the world's greatest literature and the greatest record of spiritual questing. Prayer is fellowship with God, and we can

77

scarcely afford to neglect it if we would find him. The spirit of man is the lamp of the Lord[10]; the more such light shines on us from other persons, the more we sense our need of light. "If any man would come after me," said Jesus, "let him deny himself, and take up his cross and follow me."[11] These are the major avenues to the discovery of God. Without a sense of their importance, it is doubtful whether anything else will do more than prick the surface of our complacent and stupefying indifference.

Repentance. We said earlier that *without a clearing away of evil there is no orderly goodness.* This means repentance for our sins. The idea of sin is something that has not been very popular, particularly in sophisticated circles, for some time. This does not mean there has been less sinning! Psychological determinism, the belief that our

10 Proverbs 20: 27.
11 Matthew 16: 24.

thoughts and acts are inevitably fixed by circumstances we cannot control, has led many to drop sin from their vocabularies and substitute "maladjustment." But an evil thing by any other name is just as evil.

It is sin that primarily separates us from God and our fullest living. The early Old Testament writers knew less psychology than we, but they grasped this fact; and the story of the fall of man in the Garden of Eden[12] is their way of stating in mythological language this eternal truth. We cannot really find God until we face our shortcomings and in humility and earnestness seek his help to put them from us. When we do, a miracle is wrought, we are born again, and God gives us power to live triumphantly through his Spirit.[13]

Without repentance there can be no forgiveness, and without forgiveness no newness

[12] Genesis 3.
[13] See John 3: 1-21.

of life. If this sounds old-fashioned, it is well to consider that psychiatry is now reinforcing what people of religious vision have long known. Until we will "face reality"—which means the ugly realities of our own lives as well as the pleasant facts of existence—get a new center of will, and as far as possible make amends for the past, there can be no mental health. There is profound psychological as well as religious insight in these words of the Communion service:

We do earnestly repent, and are heartily sorry for these, our misdoings; the remembrance of them is grievous unto us; the burden of them is intolerable. Have mercy upon us; have mercy upon us, most merciful Father; for thy Son, our Lord Jesus Christ's sake, forgive us all that is past; and grant that we may ever hereafter serve and please thee in newness of life, to the honour and glory of thy Name; through Jesus Christ our Lord.

A general confession is good, but in it lurks the danger of "acknowledging and bewailing" humanity's sins and not our own. The Catholic individual confessional supplies this self-examination, and it would be well if the Protestant churches had something like it if confidences were equally well guarded. Private confession to a trusted friend is often helpful to one's own self-searching and stabilization, and leads to counsel about future action. Public confession of personal sins is seldom to be commended. It too easily runs into bad taste and becomes a form of spiritual nudity; people sometimes gloat in an unlovely way over having a lurid "true confession" story to relate; it is not mentally healthy for the auditors.

Whether or not there is confession to some other person, there ought to be not morbid but honorable confession to anybody who has been wronged, unless it is clear that more harm will be done by airing the matter than by dropping it. Every possibility of restitution for injury ought to be faced and acted upon.

81

All sin is basically sin against God—disobedience to his will through our self-centeredness and violation of his love commandment. But this shows itself in a multitude of ways, and it may help us to discover our sin if we ask ourselves some such questions as these:

- Have I criticized anybody too harshly?
- Have I spread gossip?
- Have I lost my temper and said unkind things?
- Have I been jealous of anybody? Resentful or unforgiving?
- Have I tried to get possessions or honors that belonged to someone else?
- Have I tried to enjoy myself in ways harmful to others?
- Have I misused my body or my personality by overindulgence in something —smoking, drinking, sex?

82

- Have I been lazy or irresponsible about something I ought to do?
- Have I been dishonest or insincere?
- Have I had too much self-confidence? Or too little?
- Have I been concerned mainly about myself, my own affairs, my success and my future?
- Have I let my racial or economic prejudices lead me into unloving acts or attitudes?
- Have I been indifferent to those less privileged—the victims of poverty, hunger, disease, war, tyranny?
- Have I been indifferent or irreverent toward God?

Surrender. In looking at the conditions of religious living we saw that *without divine power there is no human achievement.* This is true in the sense that our entire existence and the world we live in depend upon God. It is true in the more specific sense that we cannot save ourselves from our sins.

Did you answer "yes" to any of the questions above? If you were honest, I suspect you had to say "yes" to several of them. Perhaps you feel like Paul, who said, "For I do not do the good I want, but the evil I do not want is what I do."[14]

If you feel this way, you need to do exactly what Paul did—submit yourself to God to receive a power not your own. In the very next chapter Paul says, "For the law of the Spirit of life in Christ Jesus has set me free from the law of sin and of death," and then he rises to a magnificent paean of spiritual triumph:

Who shall separate us from the love of Christ? Shall tribulation, or distress, or persecution, or famine, or nakedness, or peril, or sword? . . . No,

[14] Romans 7: 19.

84

in all these things we are more than conquerors through him who loved us.[15]

To make this surrender, it is necessary to confront one's specific sins—not merely one's general sinfulness—and determine by the help of God to overcome them. This crucial step is an act of will which no human being can perform for another person.

People sometimes think of surrender to God as something which blots out personality to leave one a spineless nonentity. On the contrary, it does just the opposite: it enhances one's will by giving it redirection and power. Instead of having self at the center of your life, you put God and other persons there. This means that you have new interests and new sympathies. As you throw yourself into the doing of something worth while, you forget to worry about yourself, and you find unity and poise. What psychology calls "be-

[15] Romans 8: 35-37.

coming an extrovert" is one aspect of what religion calls more richly salvation by faith.

This means becoming more unselfish and more thoughtful of others, and therefore more co-operative in matters of everyday living. But it means also becoming more heroic and far-seeing in larger group relations. The surrender which sweetens one's temper and deepens one's purpose in the relations of home, school, or place of work is very important. Yet such surrender will be gravely incomplete unless it opens your eyes and your sympathies to the need of those who are victims of an un-Christian social order, stirs in you a sense of social sin, and crystallizes effort to remove barriers to peace and justice. The larger one's vision and devotion, the more one is delivered from petty ways of living.

This process of deliverance through surrender is a paradoxical freedom. One gives up the freedom of self-will to find a higher freedom. This is stated accurately in the hymn:

> Make me a captive, Lord,
> And then I shall be free.

It was stated immortally by Jesus in the paradox of losing one's life to find it.[16] It is the meaning of living in him "in whose service is perfect freedom."

There is no uniform way in which this new life expresses itself. According to your temperament, you may feel a great wave of emotional exaltation; or you may simply feel that you have a depth and steadiness of purpose you did not have before; or you yourself may be less aware of change than are others who note the transformation in you. God does not run us all into one mold in the deep things of religion any more than he does in the rest of our living.

[16] Matthew 10: 39; 16: 25; Mark 8: 35; Luke 9: 24; John 12: 25.

You must in some definite way express your determination, or you will lose it. The older forms of evangelism made much of going forward to the altar, standing, or raising one's hand as a public declaration. This has the limitation of making too public—too much a matter of curiosity for others—what ought to be an inner and holy matter. The signing of a card is less objectionable, provided it does not become a mere formality. The best way is to make to your friends and to your pastor a simple, natural statement—not forced or "staged" in any way—of the new light that has come to you and the new resolves you have formed. The last thing in the world which ought to happen is for the most sacred things of life to become theatrical or mechanical.[17]

[17] Evangelists have been known to make the mistake of telling, or even boasting, how many souls they have won to Christ. Nobody ever "wins souls" without the way having been prepared by many, and such matters are best regarded with reverent humility.

When through response to some high stimulus, repentance, and surrender of will you have found God to be present with you as a living reality, there is a temptation to feel that now you have "got religion" and the process is over. It is never over. Until the end of your days the Christian life will remain both an achievement and a quest. Without growth through action, what has been born in you will surely die. How best to nourish it will be our next inquiry.

CHAPTER FOUR

GROWTH IN POWER

The preceding chapter gave some suggestions for opening one's life to the presence and power of God. But like Commencement when one graduates from school, what may seem like an end is really only a beginning. It is what comes afterward that determines how much ground has been gained.

The last of the four conditions for religious living was this: *Without action there is no growth.* Let us see what this means in several spheres.

Problems of Moral Living

A new power to live in the light of God's Spirit does not mean that you have ceased to sin. You will have to put to yourself again and again such questions as those on pages 82, 83 and repeatedly in penitence ask God for cleansing. But if you persist you will be able, like many generations of Christians before you, to "grow in the grace and knowledge of our Lord and Savior Jesus Christ."[1] This means that as you measure yourself more and more by Christ, you will see sins you did not before suspect you had. This is as it should be, for such awareness will be the growing pains of an increasingly sensitive conscience.

Two things in particular may trouble you. One is to break the power of habit, the other to know what God's will is.

Habit. Habits are so much a part of us

[1] II Peter 3: 18.

91

that even a real religious awakening will not wholly break their hold. The particular habits you will need most to be aware of are those which have worked their way into attitudes of will so that selfishness, snobbishness, fault-finding, laziness, jealousy, self-delusion, and the like have become chronic.

There are four things you must do about them. (1) Think about yourself until you discover what is the matter. (2) Set your mind on a positive attitude or action which corresponds to each of your bad ones. (3) Act on this as soon and as often as you can. (4) Throughout, ask God's help and follow his leading. If you fail the first time—or many times—keep on trying. To try and fail and try again is far less disgraceful than not to make an attempt. Remember it was the same Peter who denied his Lord because he could not stand a serving-maid's taunting, who rallied the disciples so that the Christian church could be established.[2] In his great sermon at Pentecost he quoted,

I will pour out my Spirit upon all flesh . . .
and your young men shall see visions,
and your old men shall dream dreams.[3]

This gives the key to his power—and ours— to surmount evil tendencies imbedded in both flesh and spirit.

Knowledge of God's Will. To know the will of God in some things is clear enough. You know that you ought not to kill or to commit adultery, to lie, or steal, or cheat. But other matters are less clear. Should you accept an office which will give you honor but take time and strength needed for your other work? Should you use money for an education that your family needs for something else? Should you marry a person of different religion, or of no religion? Should you change

2 Matthew 26: 69-75; Acts 2.
3 Acts 2: 17, quoted from Joel 2: 28.

your job? Life is full of such questions which no formal code will settle for us.

In such issues there are three things to do. The first is to pray, as sincerely and simply as you can, for God's light and God's leading. If you do this persistently and earnestly, tangled issues will assume order, and you will see things in clearer perspective.

The second is to examine the whole issue in the light of the supreme moral teaching of Jesus. When you do this it becomes apparent that nothing you can *have* in the way of money, honors, comforts, or pleasures is so important as what you *are*. This will settle many questions as to what is most important to the self you will always have to live with. When real values in your own life and another's conflict, you are less likely to be wrong if you act unselfishly, though there are occasions when you ought not to sacrifice a great value such as an education, or the time you need for something important, in order to give someone else a lesser value.

The third thing to do (and it must be done in conjunction with the second, not after it) is to survey the whole situation in the light of the probable consequences. You cannot foresee them all; but by recalling your own experience and observing that of others you can usually see clearly enough the probable outcome. You need to be very careful not to deceive yourself, for it is easy to look only at the side of the case which supports one's desires. The chief service a counselor can render is to help you to see these wider implications, such as, for example, that few marriages turn out well unless based upon deep common loyalties. If a counselor is wise, he will not make your decision for you, and you should not ask him to do so.

Prayer is no substitute for these other requirements. God expects us in every decision to use our own best intelligence, and any idea

95

that God's guidance excuses us from this does much harm. But neither is intelligence a substitute for prayer.

Prayer and Private Worship

All sincere Christians at times feel like saying as the disciples did to Jesus, "Lord, teach us to pray."[4] It is so difficult, yet so vital, an art that one feels baffled before it.

Like any other art, it is impossible to reduce it to rules. To do so would make it a technique and not an art. But there are certain principles to observe.

First, *prayer must be centered upon God.* The Lord's Prayer begins with an act of adoration. The psalmist wrote, "I keep the Lord always before me."[5] Anyone who does not do this is not praying—he is simply rearranging his own thoughts. But it is not enough to begin with some formula of adora-

[4] Luke 11: 1.
[5] Psalms 16: 8.

tion or thanksgiving. You must feel your own littleness before God's greatness: you must genuinely feel grateful and receptive. To enter into this mood, it is helpful to think over your blessings and your own shortcomings. Then self-searching and petition fall into their rightful places, and you can ask God to help you in anything of importance to you. It does not matter greatly about the sequence or form in which the words shape themselves. The less you think about that, the better. But it matters much that God be put foremost in your attitudes.

Second, *prayer must be natural*. This means that some people pray best in forms familiar through long experience and others through petitions framed anew on each occasion. You have to discover in which way you can do it most readily. Variation is helpful—pray sometimes by using memorized prayers, sometimes thoughtfully read a prayer from some good collection,[6] sometimes shape your own. No prayer made up by another will touch your life in everything, for no one else has exactly your experience and your needs. Yet the experience of others—particularly in the great prayers used by the Church for centuries—will help you as your own grows. You need especially to be on guard lest prayer become merely a mechanical repetition of words. The moment you find this happening, change to some other form.

Third, *prayer must be unhurried*. This does not mean that it must be long drawn out. Most of the great Christians I know are very busy people. There is danger of being so busy even about good works that God gets pushed out. To keep God at the center of one's life requires frequent renewal of power through prayer. But such renewal is not measured by the amount of time it takes,

[6] See list on page 124.

rather by the degree to which one is able even for a short time to have relaxed and unhurried communion with God. One can pray inwardly at any time and anywhere—in a subway or on an athletic field. But one prays best either alone or with understanding friends. To avoid neglecting to pray, it is best to have a time-habit and a place-habit. This is so important that it is worth great effort, in spite of the hurry of life and our lack of privacy.

Fourth, *prayer must be intellectually sincere.* It is a mistake to try to pray to a God you think does not exist, or to pray for something you think cannot possibly happen. This does not mean you should stop praying if you have some doubts. Often, to pray is the best way to get the personal depth of religious insight before which your doubts will flee away. But if prayer seems a "hollow mockery," do not go on letting it mock you. Get a book and read what some wise person whom you trust says about it.[7] Decide whether you agree with him. Then pray according to whatever framework of belief seems to you satisfying. Do *not* try to philosophize while you are praying, for you cannot have a spiritually receptive and an intellectually analytical attitude at the same time. There is need for analysis before and after, but to try to analyze while you are praying is ruinous. Stop praying infantile prayers addressed to an elderly gentleman in the sky if possibly you have been doing so, and pray with emotional and intellectual maturity.

Fifth, *prayer must combine alertness with passivity.* While you are praying, you ought not to work too hard at it. To do so is to screw yourself into a tension which prevents being receptive—and receptivity is of the essence of prayer. But neither ought you to relax so much that you fall asleep, or into

[7] See list on page 122.

a daydream. Praying is not *strenuous*, but it is *serious* business.

Sixth, *prayer must be accompanied by active effort*. It is a very irreligious attitude to pray and expect God to do all the work. There may be situations, as in serious illness, when there is nothing more you can do. At such times, to pray and then in calmness to leave the outcome to God is the best procedure. But almost always you can do something. In illness, to pray and not to give adequate medical care would be unwise and unethical. The same holds everywhere else. You need to pray for wisdom and strength for your own remaking, and then set yourself to it. You need to pray for others and set yourself to helping them. Some people do not believe in praying for other people, but it is a Christian expression of our concern and is required of us both for what it may lead to in itself and as a stimulus to our service.

Finally, *prayer must be based on intelligent trust.* This means that you ought not to pray for things which God cannot give you without upsetting his laws or doing contradictory things. This does not forbid you to pray for essential material things, for "daily bread" is an important part of life. But it probably will not come to you miraculously, and you should not expect it to do so. It is far more important to pray for strength and courage to accept deprivation with spirit undaunted than to pray for the specific things you want. The greatest prayer ever uttered was one spoken in a garden, ". . . nevertheless, not as I will, but as thou wilt."[8] Every petition should be made in this spirit. What matters supremely in prayer is that God be exalted and that you be brought to a life-transforming willingness to follow his way.

[8] Matthew 26: 39; Mark 14: 36; Luke 22: 42.

Devotional Literature

Your private worship will be most fruitful if you unite with it some reading of great religious literature. This will help both to guide your thoughts into concrete channels and lead you to share something of the feeling the authors had.

The Bible. For this purpose there is no greater book than the Bible. Since this is a compilation of books of many kinds, you will find in it something for many moods. It is not all of equal value, and you will not get the most out of it if you try to read it through as if it were all on one level. It is a record, extending over many centuries, of the growing experience of a people and of their search for God. It reflects in some places the crude scientific and ethical concepts of its authors. It was never written as a textbook in history, and there are contradictions in it which make it impossible to take it all literally. Nevertheless, if you read it for what it is meant to be—a many-sided expression of religious experience—it will be immensely helpful to your own experience. The problem of biblical interpretation is too large an issue to go into here, but a few principles for using the Bible may be suggested.

As soon as possible, get an understanding of its general sequence and structure. Learn what was written first and what next, what caused the books to come into being, what sort of literature they are. You will not want to do this while you are worshiping, but you need to do it for your general cultural knowledge. There is an appalling biblical illiteracy among those who think themselves educated. When you have this framework in mind, you can use the Bible both more intelligently and more worshipfully. Take a course in it, if you can, but if not consult some of the books listed in the Bibliography.[9]

[9] See page 125.

Occasionally, read a whole book through at one time. Perhaps you know the poem by Anna Hempstead Branch:

For a great wind blows through Ezekiel and John,
They are all one flesh that the spirit breathes upon.[10]

You can scarcely fail to feel a great wind blowing through you if you read a book of the Bible in a receptive mood. Read it leisurely enough to let its beauty and depth get hold of you, but do not slow up to puzzle over each hard passage. There is another time for that.

For your daily period of worship read only a few verses and think about them. Think what they must have meant to the people who wrote them, or about whom they are written. Then apply them to yourself, and

[10] From the poem, "In the Beginning Was the Word," in *The Third Book of Modern Verse,* compiled by Jessie B. Rittenhouse (Boston: Houghton Mifflin Company, 1927).

see what they suggest to you of challenge or comfort or illumination. For this purpose, the most fruitful parts of the Bible are the Psalms, the Gospels, and the New Testament letters. However, you will find passages of great beauty and power all through. Whenever you come across these, mark them for future reference. If you have a lurking notion that to mark your Bible is irreverent, dispel it.

Use whatever devotional aids you find helpful. But do not depend upon them. It is much more valuable to compile your own list of beautiful and meaningful passages, making a note perhaps of what they suggest to you, than to follow any ready-made list. As a start, you might look up the passages referred to in the footnotes of this book.

Memorize some of the deathless passages of the Bible. Our fathers used to commit them to memory much more than we do. It is unfortunate both for religion and for contemporary culture that this practice has lapsed.

Other Devotional Literature. I shall not say much about other reading, for there is much which passes as devotional literature that I find more irritating than helpful. It too often oozes unctuousness. However, there are some famous classics of the soul which people of all ages have found helpful. Among these are St. Augustine's *Confessions*, Thomas à Kempis' *Imitation of Christ*, and Brother Lawrence's *Practice of the Presence of God*. A modern classic of rich spiritual meaning is Thomas R. Kelly's *Testament of Devotion*. Also, there is great religious literature outside of the Christian tradition, and you will find many high thoughts in Plato's *Apology* or *Phaedo* and Marcus Aurelius' *Meditations*. Such an anthology as the *Treasure House of the World's Religions*[11] may be used occasionally both for variety and for the in-

[11] Compiled by Robert E. Hume.

sights it will give you into the religious aspirations of those who have sought God through different channels. There are collections of great religious poetry available[12] which should stir you to worship as well as to feel their beauty. Those which you like best should be memorized.

There are some modern compilations for daily readings which are excellent. It is impossible to prescribe for another, for tastes differ. Try out some of those listed in the Bibliography[13]; if they appeal to you, stay by them, and if not, use something else. In general, the principles by which to judge such materials are these: (1) Do they have religious sincerity and depth? (2) Are they good literature? (3) Do they stir your aspiration and impel you to action?

[12] See page 125.
[13] See page 124.

The Church

Some people who have respect for religion and a sense of its importance do not have much regard for the Church. Often they neither enjoy going to church nor see much reason that one should go. Let us ask first *how* one should attend church, and this may throw light on *why*.

How to Attend Church. Our church services are not by any means all that they ought to be. One finds there poor preaching, bad music, antiquated theology, ugly architecture, hypocritical people, almost anything you wish to say. But one finds there also sincerity, beauty, devotion, depth, earnestness about God and goodness. What you find in a church depends in part (though not wholly) on what you look for.

The first principle for attending church is to go in a receptive and appreciative, not in a critical, attitude. The fault-finding spirit will drive out the worshiping attitude more quickly than will anything else, and it is hardly fair then to blame the church for not leading you into worship. It is the same as with friendships: the more you pick flaws in people from the outside, the less you get into the inside of their lives.

A second requirement is to shut distractions from your mind. You may not be able to do this wholly. But remember you are there to *worship*—not to look around at people's clothes, or go over in your mind what you did last night, or plan out your week's work. There are other occasions for such matters.

A third is to enter into all the hymns and responses. There is little enough opportunity in a church service for personal participation, but people often cut themselves off from what there is by passively looking on.

Fourth, you should, if possible, connect yourself with the work of the church in some

way other than attending the Sunday service.
You need to do this for the help you can give,
but you also need to do it in order to feel
yourself a part of it. One large reason that
students who were active in the church in
their home communities drift away from it in
college is that there they were active and
at college they are often merely onlookers.

Fifth, you ought, if you are free to do so,
to choose the church best suited to your
temperament. When you have been reared
in a certain church and have many ties there,
it is usually unwise to break them. But if you
are in a new environment where you are free
to choose, attend the church where you find
you can worship best. There are three general types of worship. As its main feature,
one has silence, one has liturgy, one has the
sermon. Most people do not know what to do
with silence, and this is why it is not often
found outside of the Society of Friends. We
should cultivate further its power, both pri-

vately and in group worship. A liturgical
service, such as the Roman Catholic or
Episcopalian, offers beauty and dignity, and
is usually superior in its union of aesthetic
with religious values. The service built
around the sermon, with which the majority
of Protestants are most familiar, has more of
moral content than either of the others. It
is a mistake, however, to judge a service
wholly by the sermon—as if nothing else mat-
tered. We go to church primarily to worship
God, not primarily to listen to a discourse,
and even a poor sermon can give us the occasion to enter into the presence of God.

Why One Attends Church. There are
various reasons that one should go to church.
One of these is that if you do not attend—
and not merely attend but enter into its on-
going life—you are a parasite! The Church is
the chief conserver of spiritual values, and
it is the institutional embodiment of our
Christian heritage. During the Dark Ages it

preserved not only religion but civilization; it has fostered the spread of education throughout the centuries; it has nourished the spirit of democracy; it has built moral attitudes into the lives of millions of persons; it has made people more humane in their treatment of the weak and underprivileged; it has goaded consciences to abolish slavery; it has lifted the position of women and children. We are the inheritors of this freedom and this humanization, in which the Church has not been the sole but has been the chief agent. To turn our backs on it is to cast off our cultural parentage.

A second reason that you need to go to church is that the Church needs you. Every criticism which can be brought against it is true—in some places and in some respects. But a very large reason that the Church is not in better health is that many persons have shunned it because it was sick. Its major need is for active and intelligent leadership.

in congregations as in pulpits. It has done great things; it can do greater. Criticism comes best from those who appreciate its value and who are working from the inside to improve it.

The basic reason for attending church is that it offers you corporate worship of God in the name of Christ. Churches are not cinemas, soda fountains, or concert halls, and are not to be judged by the amount of entertainment they provide. They are places for worship, for the nourishing of the good life, and for Christian fellowship. Conceivably one might maintain a growing religious experience without the Church—especially with some other religious organization as a substitute. But not many people do. Among a hundred who say they are going to worship in nature or at home on Sunday morning, there is perhaps one who does. Instead of asking, "Does one need to go to church to be a Christian?" one might better say, "If one is a Christian, will he want to stay away?"

Service to Other Persons

The last topic to be considered is a requirement so obvious that not much need be said about it, though one may think about it and live by it for a lifetime without probing its deep places.

The greatest words ever spoken are those of Jesus:

You shall love the Lord your God with all your heart, and with all your soul, and with all your mind. This is the great and first commandment. And a second is like it, You shall love your neighbor as yourself.[14]

On these two commandments hang not only all of the law and the prophets, but the whole of religious living. And notice that they are in integrated union. Jesus never thought of severing them.

14 Matthew 22: 37-39.

115

As you serve you grow, and you will not grow unless you serve. But if you did it *in order to grow,* you would not be acting in the spirit of Jesus. You would be using people for your ends. And this he never did. I find no evidence that he ever served others in order to do good to himself. With this fundamental fact in mind, there are two matters at which we must briefly look.

The first is the Christian's obligation to win others to Christ. When a great, new, enlarging experience has come to you, it is a natural and wholesome impulse to want to share it. The gospel means "good news," and good news needs to be told—especially when there is so much bad news in the world.

But there are certain conditions to be interposed. We have seen how religion deals with the most intimate and sacred aspects of living. To approach another about his religion may quite legitimately arouse his resentment if he thinks you are trespassing on private ground. Other persons need to be stirred to open their closed lives to God; but the way to do it is not to throw baseballs at the door of another's inner life, or shout at him to come out.

The thing for you to do is, as naturally as possible, to "live your religion," and speak about it when the occasion is fitting. There are many opportunities if one watches for them. But about the worst thing you could do would be to set out to win others to Christ without manifesting in your living that Christ has won you.

The other matter—great enough so that you must read about it in many books, hear about it in many addresses, act upon it on many occasions—is the need of fundamental social change. Poverty, class cleavage, race prejudice, war—these and many other evil things keep this from being a Christian world. The abundant life[15] that Jesus came to bring to

[15] John 10: 10.

117

every man requires courageous, intelligent, persistent effort against entrenched prejudice and power. This day, perhaps more than any former day since Christianity began, calls for a crusading spirit among those brave enough and strong enough and loving enough to work for the way of Christ in the world.

The social struggle to create a more Christian world, if taken seriously, will lead you into ways of unpopularity and loneliness where only the person whose life is grounded in God finds power to stand. If you would "take your share of suffering as a good soldier of Christ Jesus,"[16] you must find your strength where Jesus found it. But in turn, the resolute Christian quest for a better world will lead you into a deeper experience of God, and you will find God among those with whom you labor. To experience this union of challenge and power, of commitment to tasks and en-

[16] II Timothy 2: 3.

richment of life, one must pray as did Ignatius Loyola:

Teach us, good Lord, to serve Thee as Thou deservest; to give and not to count the cost; to fight and not to heed the wounds; to toil and not to seek for rest; to labor and not to ask for any reward, save that of knowing that we do Thy will; through Jesus Christ our Lord.

When Paul wrote to encourage his fellow Christians in the difficult enterprise of religious living, he closed each letter with a word commending them to a greater power than he or they. He used various forms, but what he always said was, "The grace of the Lord Jesus Christ be with you." This is what any person who would find a religion to live by needs most.

SELECTED BIBLIOGRAPHY

Books on Religious Belief

Bosley, Harold A., *A Firm Faith for Today* (New York: Harper, 1950).

Buttrick, George A., *So We Believe, So We Pray* (New York and Nashville: Abingdon-Cokesbury, 1951).

DeWolf, L. Harold, *A Theology of the Living Church* (New York: Harper, 1953).

Finegan, Jack, *Beginnings in Theology* (New York: Association Press, 1956).

Fosdick, Harry Emerson, *The Three Meanings: Prayer, Faith [and] Service* (New York: Association Press, 1950).

Gray, Henry David, *A Theology for Christian Youth* (New York and Nashville: Abingdon-Cokesbury, 1941).

Harkness, Georgia, *Conflicts in Religious Thought*, rev. ed. (New York: Harper, 1949).

———, *Understanding the Christian Faith* (New York and Nashville: Abingdon-Cokesbury, 1947).

Harner, Nevin C., *I Believe* (Philadelphia: Christian Education Press, 1950).

Hordern, William, *A Layman's Guide to Protestant Theology* (New York: Macmillan, 1955).

Jones, Rufus M., *Pathways to the Reality of God* (New York: Macmillan, 1931).

——, *A Call to What Is Vital* (New York: Macmillan, 1948).

Nichols, James H., *Primer for Protestants* (New York: Association Press, 1947).

Rall, Harris Franklin, *A Faith for Today* (New York: Abingdon, 1936).

Sockman, Ralph W., *How to Believe* (Garden City, N. Y.: Doubleday, 1953).

Spurrier, William A., *A Guide to the Christian Faith* (New York: Scribner, 1952).

Van Dusen, Henry P., *Life's Meaning* (New York: Association Press, 1951).

Books on Prayer and Worship

Bowman, Clarice, *Restoring Worship* (New York and Nashville: Abingdon-Cokesbury, 1951).

Bro, Marguerite Harmon, *More Than We Are* (New York: Harper, 1948).

Buttrick, George A., *Prayer* (New York and Nashville: Abingdon-Cokesbury, 1942).

Casteel, John L., *Rediscovering Prayer* (New York: Association Press, 1955).

Day, Albert E., *An Autobiography of Prayer* (New York: Harper, 1952).

Ferré, Nels F. S., *Strengthening the Spiritual Life* (New York: Harper, 1951).

——, *Making Religion Real* (New York: Harper, 1955).

Harkness, Georgia, *Prayer and the Common Life* (New York and Nashville: Abingdon-Cokesbury, 1948).

Kelly, Thomas R., *A Testament of Devotion* (New York: Harper, 1941).

Radcliffe, Lynn J., *Making Prayer Real* (New York and Nashville: Abingdon-Cokesbury, 1952).

Steere, Douglas V., *Prayer and Worship* (New York: Association Press, 1938).

——, *On Beginning from Within* (New York: Harper, 1943).

Whiston, Charles F., *Teach Us to Pray* (Boston: Pilgrim Press, 1949).

Wyon, Olive, *The School of Prayer* (Philadelphia: Westminster, 1944).

Devotional Manuals and Collections of Prayers

Book of Common Prayer

Baillie, John, *A Diary of Private Prayer* (New York: Scribner, 1936).

Clark, Thomas Curtis, *Today Is Mine* (New York: Harper, 1950).

Cushman, Ralph S., *Hilltop Verses and Prayers* (New York and Nashville: Abingdon-Cokesbury, 1945).

Harkness, Georgia, *Through Christ Our Lord* (New York and Nashville: Abingdon-Cokesbury, 1950).

——, *Be Still and Know* (New York and Nashville: Abingdon-Cokesbury, 1953).

Jones, E. Stanley, *Abundant Living* (New York and Nashville: Abingdon-Cokesbury, 1942).

Oldham, J. H. *Devotional Diary* (New York: Harper, 1931).

Orchard, W. E., *The Temple* (New York: Dutton, 1918).

Rauschenbusch, Walter, *Prayers of the Social Awakening* (Boston: Pilgrim Press, 1910, 1925).

Student Prayerbook, The (New York: Association Press, 1953).

Tileston, Mary W., *Prayers Ancient and Modern* (New York: Grosset and Dunlap, 1897, 1928).

Willett, Herbert L., and C. C. Morrison, *The Daily Altar* (New York: Harper, 1918).

Wilson, Hazel T., *Prayers for Living* (New York and Nashville: Abingdon-Cokesbury, 1955).

Anthologies of Religious Poetry

Albertson, C. C., *Lyra Mystica* (New York: Macmillan, 1932).

Hill, Caroline M., *The World's Great Religious Poetry* (New York: Macmillan, 1923).

Morrison, James D., *Masterpieces of Religious Verse* (New York: Harper, 1948).

Nicholson, D. H. S., and A. H. E. Lee, *The Oxford Book of English Mystical Verse* (New York: Oxford University Press, 1917).

Books on the Bible

There are hundreds of these. Among the simplest and most helpful are:

Anderson, Bernhard, *Rediscovering the Bible* (New York: Association Press, 1951).

Blair, Edward P., *The Bible and You* (New York and Nashville: Abingdon-Cokesbury, 1953).

125

Bowie, W. R., *The Story of the Bible* (New York: Abingdon-Cokesbury, 1935).

Chase, Mary Ellen, *The Bible and the Common Reader* (New York: Macmillan, 1944).

Fosdick, Harry Emerson, *The Modern Use of the Bible* (New York: Macmillan, 1924, 1940).

——, *A Guide to Understanding the Bible* (New York: Harper, 1938).

Goodspeed, Edgar J., *The Story of the Bible* (Chicago: University of Chicago Press, 1936). (Old and New Testaments are also available separately.)

Harkness, Georgia, *Toward Understanding the Bible* (New York: Scribner, 1954).

Laymon, Charles M., *The Life and Teachings of Jesus* (New York and Nashville: Abingdon-Cokesbury, 1955).

Love, Julian P., *How to Read the Bible* (New York: Macmillan, 1945).

Mould, Elmer W. K., *Essentials of Bible History*, rev. ed. (New York: Ronald Press, 1951).

Neil, William, *The Rediscovery of the Bible* (New York: Harper, 1954).

Parmelee, Alice, *A Guidebook to the Bible* (New York: Harper, 1948).

Watts, Harold H., *The Modern Reader's Guide to the Bible* (New York: Harper, 1949).